Milet Publishing
Smallfields Cottage, Cox Green
Rudgwick, Horsham, West Sussex
RH12 3DE England
info@milet.com
www.milet.com
www.milet.co.uk

First English–Korean edition published by Milet Publishing in 2013

Copyright © Milet Publishing, 2013

ISBN 978 1 84059 827 8

Original Turkish text written by Erdem Seçmen
Translated to English by Alvin Parmar and adapted by Milet

Illustrated by Chris Dittopoulos
Designed by Christangelos Seferiadis

Printed and bound in Turkey by Ertem Matbaası

My Bilingual Book

Taste
맛보기

English–Korean

Close your eyes, taste this drink . . .

눈을 감고 이 음료수를 맛보세요 . . .

Water or soda, what do you think?

물이나 사이다, 어떠세요?

How do you know which one it is?

물이고 사이다인지 어떻게 아세요?

Do your mouth and tongue feel a fizz?

입과 혀에서 쉬하는 소리를 느끼세요?

Your mouth and tongue let you taste drinks and food.

여러분은 입과 혀로 음료수와 음식의 맛을 볼 수 있습니다.

They tell you what tastes bad and what tastes good!

입과 혀는 어떤 맛이 나쁘고 어떤 맛이 좋은지 말해줍니다!

Your taste senses bitter, sour, sweet,

여러분이 느끼는 맛은 크래커처럼 쓰고, 시고,

and salty, like the crackers you eat.

달고, 짠 것입니다.

Some like the taste of chocolate best.

일부는 초콜릿 맛처럼 최고이고, 대부분은 약

Most like the taste of medicine less!

맛처럼 안 좋습니다!

It's fun to think about yummy sweets,

달콤한 과자를 생각하는 것을 재미있지만, 너무

but eating too many is bad for your teeth!

많이 먹으면 치아에 나쁩니다!

Foods like peppers can be so hot!

고추 같은 음식은 매우 매울 수 있습니다!

Your taste will tell you to eat them or not.

여러분의 맛은 먹어야 할지 여부를 말해줍니다.

Some tastes go together and some really don't mix,

일부 맛들은 합쳐지고 일부는 정말로 합쳐지지 않는데,

like that banana and cheese sandwich you are about to fix!

마치 만들려고 하는 바나나 치즈 샌드위치와 같은 경우입니다!

These delicious fruits deserve a nibble.

이 맛있는 과일들은 한입 깨물어 볼만합니다.

They're good for your body and irresistible!

그것들은 몸에 좋으니 거부할 수 없죠!

Trying different foods makes your taste sense grow.

다른 음식들을 먹어보면 여러분은 맛보는 감각을 높일 수 있습니다.

Your world gets bigger, the more foods that you know!

여러분의 세계가 커지면 커질수록, 더 많은 음식들을 알게 됩니다!